The
VIKING
Library

Viking Longships

Andrea Hopkins, Ph.D.

The Rosen Publishing Group's
PowerKids Press™
New York

To the memory of my friend Egil Kristoffersen, who shared with me
his vast knowledge and understanding of the Vikings, and showed me some of their ships

Published in 2002 by The Rosen Publishing Group, Inc.
29 East 21st Street, New York, NY 10010

First Edition.

Book Design and Layout: Michael Caroleo

Project Editor: Frances E. Ruffin

Photo Credits: Title page, p. 7 © Werner Forman Archive; contents page © Walter Bibiko/The Viesti Collection; pp. 4, 12 (bottom),
15 © Mary Evans Picture Library; pp. 8 (left), 12 (top right) © AKG London; pp. 8 (right), 20 Statens Historiska Museum and Universitets
Oldsaksamling; p. 11 © SuperStock; 12 (top left) © York Archeological Studies; p. 16 (left) © Bettmann/CORBIS; pp. 16 (right),
19 © North Wind Pictures.

Hopkins, Andrea.
    Viking longships / Andrea Hopkins
            p. cm. — (The Vikings)
Includes index
    ISBN 0-8239-5812-4 (lib. bdg.)
    1. Vikings—Juvenile literature. 2. Viking ships—Juvenile
literature. [1. Vikings. 2. Ships] I. Title
    DL65 .H69 2001
    948' .022—dc21

                                        00-011280

Manufactured in the United States of America

Contents

1 The Viking Age Begins 5

2 Who Were the Vikings? 6

3 How the Vikings Loved Their Ships 9

4 Ships for Different Purposes 10

5 Building a Longship 13

6 A Fit Viking Ship 14

7 A Viking Business 17

8 Living Aboard a Longship 18

9 A Queen Is Buried 21

10 Vikings on the Open Sea 22

Glossary 23

Index 24

Web Sites 24

For centuries, the appearance of Viking longships frightened people in Europe and in other parts of the world. The painting shows Viking ships on the North Sea.

The Viking Age Begins

On June 8th, A.D. 793, several longships sailed up to Lindisfarne, a **monastery** in England. Out of the ships came many strangers. They were Norsemen, armed with swords and shields and wearing helmets. Some **monks** stepped forward to greet the strangers and to ask them what they wanted. The strange men drew their swords and killed the monks. To the horror of other monks who had been watching, the strangers ran to the monastery. They even ran inside the church. They snatched up treasures that were kept there. The strangers stole everything they could carry. They took gold and silver candlesticks, **crucifixes**, coins, and beautifully decorated books.

The men killed everyone who tried to stop them and set the church on fire. They took young, strong monks and their servants with them to sell as slaves. Then they sailed away. This was the beginning of the Viking Age, when Norsemen in their longships terrorized most of western Europe for nearly 300 years.

5

Who Were the Vikings?

Norse people lived in the countries that are now called Sweden, Norway, and Denmark. They are in **Scandinavia**, an area of northern Europe. Not all Norsemen were Vikings. To call someone a Viking was like calling that person a pirate. The word "viking" came from the Norse word "vik," meaning a bay or creek. To go "viking" meant to sail off in a longship to **raid** and steal from other people. Most Norse people were farmers, but almost everyone traveled by boat. In the 700s, there were very few towns and almost no roads. Much of the land was covered in thick, dark forest, with plenty of **timber** for building boats. Boats were almost more important to the Norse people than cars are to us.

The countries of Norway, Sweden, and Denmark, shown on the map, were the Viking homelands. The Viking ship is believed to have belonged to a Norse queen. It is on display in a Norwegian museum. ▶

Norway

Sweden

Denmark

Many Viking picture stones showed details of their longships, and they described what Vikings believed was life after death. ▶

◀ This picture stone, carved in the 800s, shows Viking warriors in a fighting ship. It also shows the sails and the shape of the longship.

How the Vikings Loved Their Ships

We can tell that the Norse people felt very strongly about their ships. Before they became **Christian**, they sometimes sank their ships as gifts to their gods. Some very rich and important people were even buried in their ships. The Norse carved ships on special stones, bits of bone, or wood, and **embroidered** them on cloth. Over time they learned to make different kinds of ships for different purposes. There were many Norse words that described their ships, and how they were built and sailed. The Norse were a strong and curious people. They used their ships to explore new places, to trade with other people, and, of course, to go viking. For Norsemen who chose to become Vikings, their ships meant freedom. They were the key to adventures that might lead either to riches or death.

Ships for Different Purposes

Viking trading ships were wide in the middle with space for goods. They had flatter bottoms than warships and could sail down even shallow rivers. Vikings could land anywhere because their ships were able to come close to a beach. Other ships needed a harbor with a pier.

As time went by, Vikings built ships of different sizes, shapes, designs, and for different purposes. They could sail down shallow rivers or across the open ocean. Most Viking longships were smaller, lighter, and moved faster than ships used by people in other parts of Europe. Each Viking longship could change the position of its sail, so that it could move in almost any direction. Viking warships were long and slender. They could move very fast. There was little room in them for anything but men and their weapons.

This painting by the American James G. Tyler (1855-1931) shows Viking longships on a stormy sea.

Building a Longship

It took many Norse **craftsmen** to build a longship. Their ships were made of pine or oak. Viking shipbuilders did not use metal saws to cut trees into timber. They split logs by driving wedges into them. They used axes to cut the logs into planks of the right length and shape. This took a lot of time and labor. Shipbuilders then fitted the **keel** of the ship into place. This huge piece of timber runs down the center of a ship. Then they built the sides of the ship with long planks called strakes. Strakes were placed one over the other like tiles on a roof. The strakes were fastened down with leather strips, wooden rods, or iron pins.

The drawing shows men repairing a longship. Pieces of twine or wool soaked in tar were stuffed between strakes to prevent water from getting through the gaps during sea voyages. The photos show the inside of a longship, and axes used long ago to build boats.

A Fit Viking Ship

The ship was steered or guided by a large, wooden rudder. This movable, flat piece of wood was at the back of the ship on the right side. The Norse word for the rudder was "styri" and the side of the ship it was fastened to was called "styrabord." Today, sailors call the right side of their ship "starboard."

A single **mast** on each Viking longship held a single, square sail. Two large, wooden blocks set into the keel held the mast upright. Ropes called rigging helped to support the mast and sail. When there was not enough wind to fill the sail, Viking seamen used oars to power their ships. These oars could be as long as 18 feet (3.5 m). The sides of some ships were high, about 5 feet (1.5 m) above the water level. Shipbuilders cut holes into the sides of a ship through which oars would be placed. These holes could be closed when not in use.

The painting and outlines are of a longship. The wooden dragon from a Viking ship was found in 1880. Vikings painted tar on their ships to prevent worms from chewing the wood. Damage from worms caused ships to sink. ▶

A Viking Business

You had to be a rich **chieftain** to own a Viking longship. They were expensive. Vikings looked on their **expeditions** to raid or trade as a business. A shipowner hired a skilled and experienced **helmsman** to **navigate** the ship. He also hired a crew of brave men. The crew of a longship agreed to obey the chieftain in exchange for shares in the profits from their expedition. The chieftain received the largest share. Vikings rarely went on raids with just one longship. It was safer to raid in small groups of at least three longships. Large **fleets** of ships, carrying armies of Vikings, raided many European countries from the ninth to the eleventh centuries.

◄ *In these paintings, a fleet of Viking raiders are landing on the coast of France. Once at sea, everyone on a ship took turns rowing, except for the helmsman.*

Living Aboard a Longship

When the Norse made very long journeys, they spent several days or even weeks onboard ship. They made careful preparations. Oatcakes were packed, along with preserved foods such as smoked meat, dried fish, or pickled fish. They took ale for drinking.

When the Norse people first used their ships for long journeys, they stayed close to the coasts. They did not venture far into the open sea, out of sight of land. If they could, they would land at night, and set up a camp on the shore. Then they lit a fire, cooked some food, and slept rolled up in their blankets. They did not make long sea journeys in winter, when the weather was really bad. The time for sailing was from April to October. A longship usually had a tent for the chieftain and his friends. Everyone else found shelter from the rain under their shields. Each man had a

Vikings respected men who could stand harsh conditions without complaining. Longships did not have decks, cabins, bunks, or hammocks. They were open to all kinds of weather.

small chest in which to store his spoon, blanket, spare clothes, and weapons. He would keep some room in it for the loot he hoped to find on the Viking raid. When he was rowing, he used his chest as a seat.

A Queen Is Buried

In 1904, a large burial mound in Oseberg, Norway was dug up. Inside it was a magnificent Viking ship full of beautiful objects, and the skeletons of two women, one old and one young. One woman may have been a queen, and the other her slave. It was impossible to tell which one was which. Valuable things—including the dead queen's jewels—had been stolen. The robbers, however, left behind important information for **archaeologists** to study. The ship was 72 feet (22 m) long, and had 15 pairs of oars. The dead queen and her slave lay surrounded by things they would need in the afterlife. There were rich **tapestries**, five beds with feather quilts, a chair, chests, oil lamps, weaving looms, pots, and food.

◄ *Photographs of a queen's Viking ship found in Oseberg, Norway, show a carriage and 2 of the 12 horse skeletons buried with the ship. Tree rings in the ship's timbers show that the ship was built around A.D. 820. The queen's burial took place in A.D. 834.*

21

Vikings on the Open Sea

Vikings watched for strong currents, or changes in the color or temperature of the sea. They looked for places where schools of fish normally swam, whales hunted, or where certain kinds of seabirds flew. All of these things could tell experienced Vikings whether or not they were close to land.

Vikings managed to sail very long distances over the dangerous, open ocean. They were excellent seamen. They measured the length of their journeys in units called dagr. This meant the distance you could sail in one day. They knew how far north or south they had traveled by the position of the sun and stars. They did not have **compasses**. When they couldn't see land, there was no way to tell their position when they sailed west or east. Vikings often made the long journey west from Norway to Iceland, all over open sea. Some Vikings sailed further west, from Iceland to Greenland. Eventually, a very few went further still, to the coast of North America.

Glossary

archaeologists (ahr-key-AH-luh-jists) Scientists who study the buildings, belongings, and other artifacts of ancient peoples.

chieftain (CHEEF-ten) The leader of a tribe, clan, or band of people.

Christian (KRIS-chun) Someone who follows the teachings of Jesus Christ and the Bible.

compasses (KUM-pus-es) Devices that are mostly used by sailors or pilots to determine direction.

craftsmen (KRAFTS-min) Skilled and creative workers.

crucifixes (KROO-suh-fiks-ez) Crosses with statues of Jesus Christ on them.

embroidered (em-BROY-durd) Stitched designs into cloth for decoration.

expeditions (ek-spuh-DIH-shunz) Trips for a special purpose.

fleets (FLEETS) Groups of warships.

helmsman (HELMZ-mun) A person who steers a ship.

keel (KEEL) The structure that runs along the bottom of a boat, from the front to the back.

mast (MAST) A long pole that rises from the keel or deck of a ship and holds its rigging and sails.

monastery (MAH-nah-ster-ee) A house where people, who have taken religious vows, live and work.

monks (MUNKS) Men who have taken religious vows and live in a monastery.

navigate (NAH-vuh-gayt) To operate or guide a ship or airplane.

raid (RAYD) A surprise attack by a group of well-armed people.

tapestries (TAH-puh-streez) Richly designed, woven fabrics used for curtains and hangings.

timber (TIM-bur) Wood that is cut and used for building houses, ships, and other wooden objects.

Scandinavia (scan-dih-NAY-vee-ah) Northern Europe, usually Norway, Sweden, and Denmark.

Index

C
chieftain, 17, 18
compasses, 22

D
Denmark, 6

E
England, 5
Europe, 6, 10, 17
expeditions, 17

G
Greenland, 22

H
helmsman, 17

I
Iceland, 22

L
Lindisfarne, 5
loot, 19

N
Norse, 6, 9, 13, 18
Norsemen, 5, 6, 9
North America, 22
Norway, 6, 21, 22

Q
queen, 21

R
raid, 6, 17, 19

S
Scandinavia, 6
shipbuilders, 13, 14
Sweden, 6

T
trade, 17

Web Sites

To learn about Viking longships, check out these Web sites:
www.pbs.org/wgbh/nova/vikings
www.sciam.com/1998/0298issue/0298hale.html

24